Teach Me Thérèse

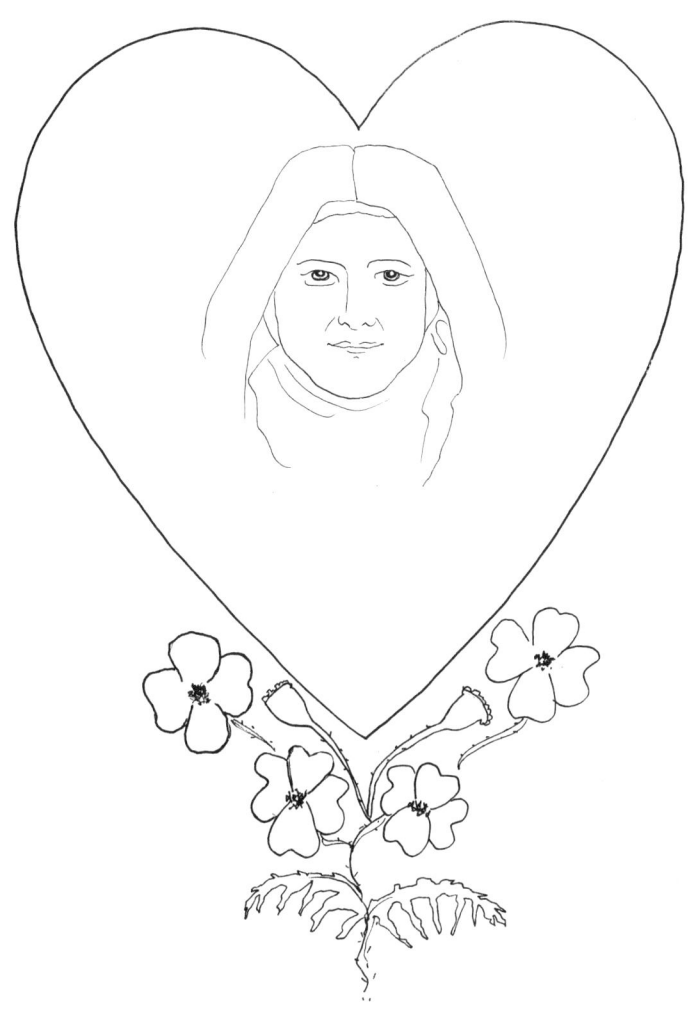

illustrated by
SUSAN BATEMAN

Second Spring Catechesis

ST THÉRÈSE, TEACH ME ABOUT YOUR LIFE.

I was born on the 2nd of January 1873.
This is me as a baby, with my mother and father and
my older sisters Marie, Pauline, Léonie and Céline.

When I was four years old my mother died and
joined my four other little brothers and sisters in heaven.
After that, my big sisters and my Papa looked after me.

This is a picture of our house in Lisieux.
It had a beautiful garden where Céline and I played.
I also liked to go fishing with Papa.

When I was ten I got very sick.
All my family were praying in front of a statue of Our Lady:
then I saw her smile at me, and I got better.

When I was thirteen Jesus gave me a wonderful
Christmas present: to become more like Him
and to love other people as much as He does.

Jesus died on the cross for us. I didn't want His suffering to go to waste, so I prayed a lot for a bad man who had murdered people. Just before he died, he kissed a crucifix to show he was sorry.

When I was fourteen, I asked my Papa if I could be a Carmelite nun. I loved Jesus so much I wanted to spend the rest of my life as close to Him as possible.

Later that year we visited the Bishop of Bayeux,
to ask if I could enter Carmel at fifteen.
He promised to think and pray about it.

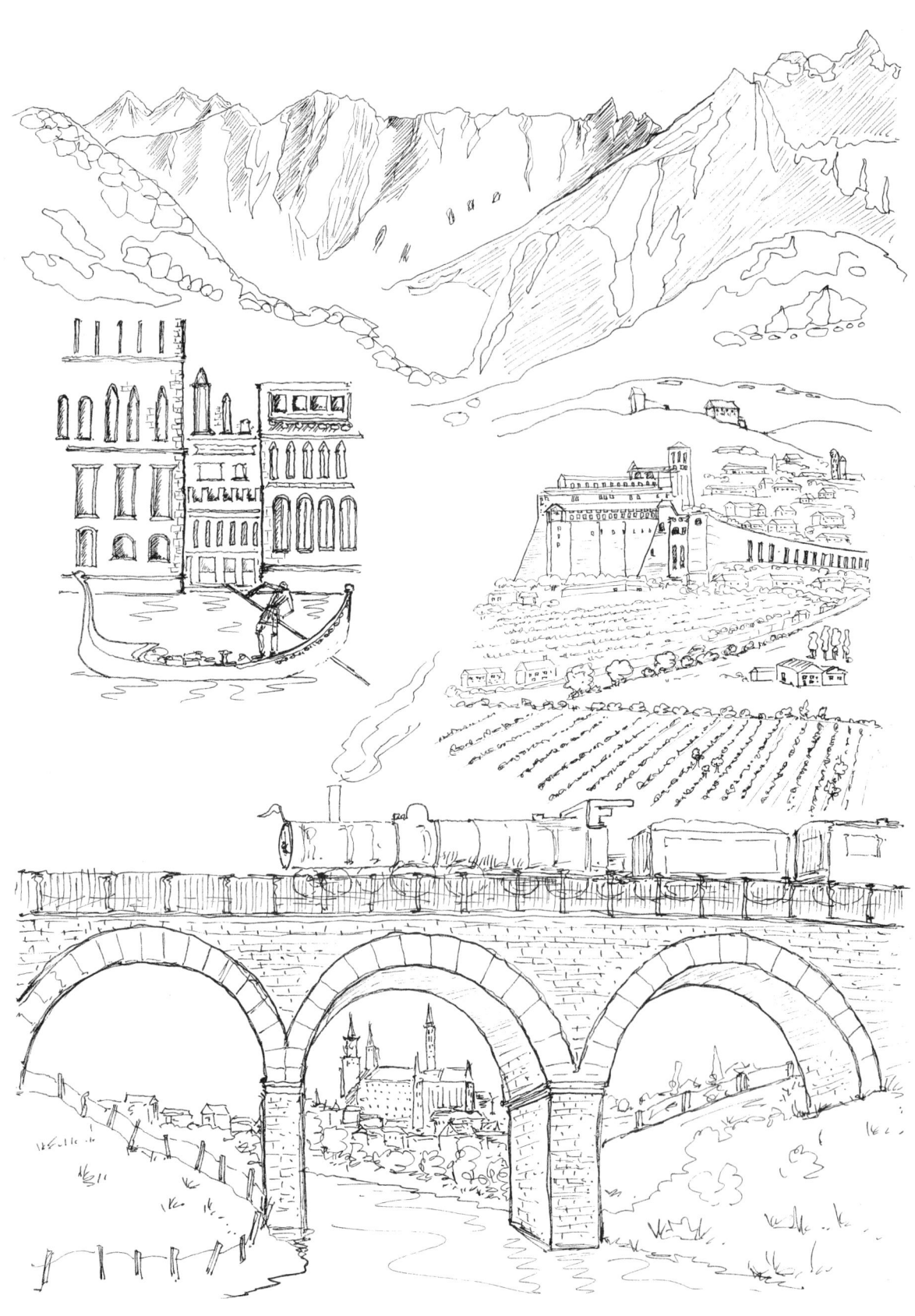

I went by train on a pilgrimage to Rome, with Papa and Céline. We passed through many beautiful and holy places on our way.

When we got to Rome, Céline and I knelt down in the Colosseum to kiss the ground where the early Christians had died for their faith.

When I was in Rome, I saw Pope Leo XIII.
He blessed me and told me that if it was God's will,
I would enter Carmel at fifteen.

At Easter, when I had turned fifteen, I did enter Carmel.
I said goodbye to my father and he blessed me
and told me that he loved me.

ST THÉRÈSE, TEACH ME ABOUT CARMEL

In Carmel we do lots of different kinds of work:
cleaning, washing, cooking and making hosts for the Mass.
We also pray and talk to Jesus all through the day.

ST THÉRÈSE, TEACH ABOUT YOUR LITTLE WAY

I entered Carmel in order to be close to Jesus, to pray for sinners and especially for priests. It makes Jesus happy when we offer to help Him, even though we can't do much. This is my 'little way' to Jesus: to trust and love Him and to let Him into your heart, where He can speak to you and tell you what He would like you to do.

ST THÉRÈSE, TEACH ME TO DO LITTLE THINGS WITH GREAT LOVE

You can show the love of God to others by paying attention to what they need and helping them cheerfully and willingly.

ST THÉRÈSE, TEACH ME TO LOOK AFTER MY PETS PROPERLY

I used to have a dog called Tom, and he was my faithful companion. When he was sick, I looked after him carefully until he got better.

ST THÉRÈSE, TEACH ME NOT TO MIND WHAT OTHER PEOPLE THINK

I wasn't always happy at school: but we can pray for people who are not kind to us.

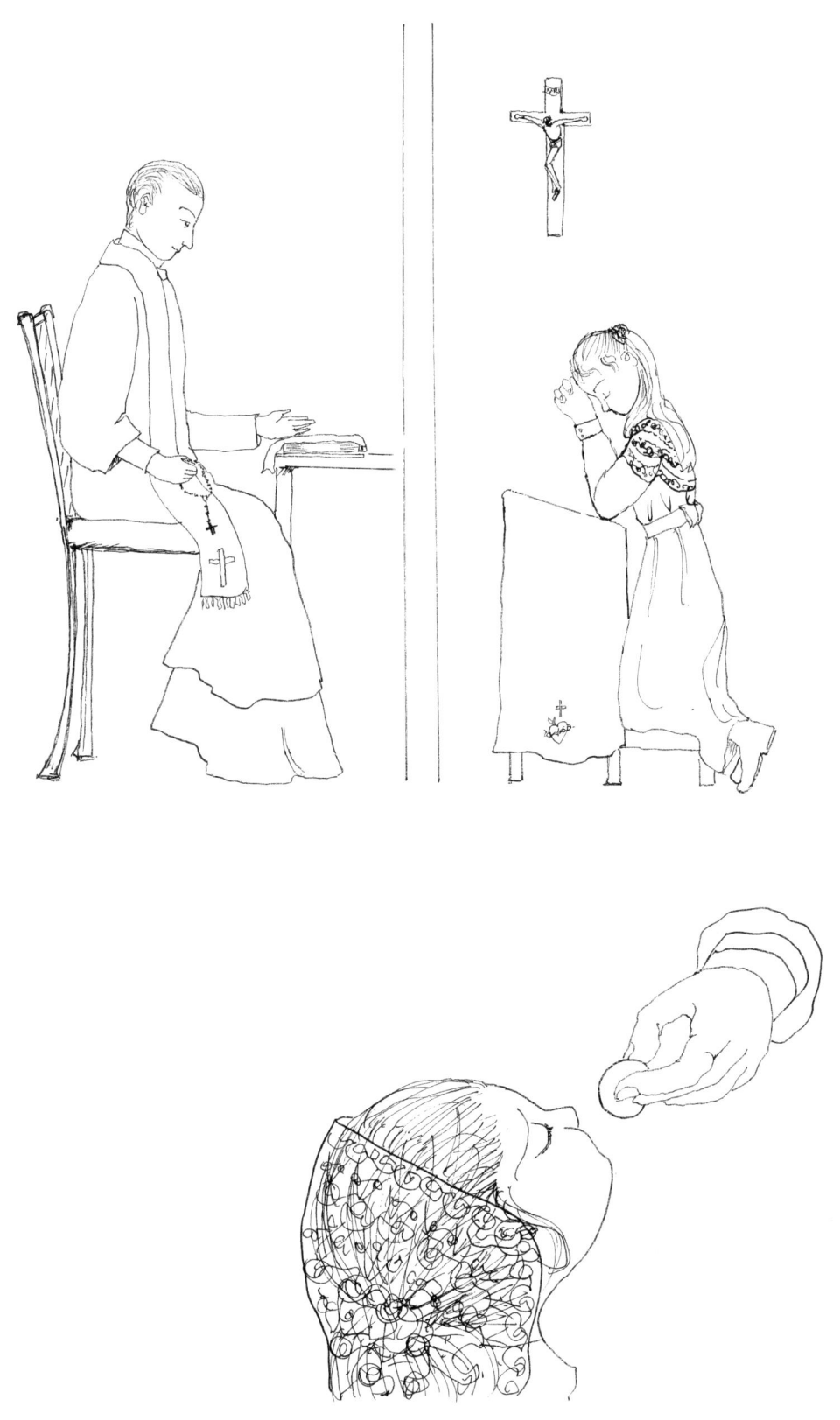

ST THÉRÈSE, TEACH ME HOW TO STAY CLOSE TO JESUS

I stayed close to Jesus by going often to confession and Mass.

ST THÉRÈSE TEACH ME TO PRAY

O my God, I ask of thee for myself
and for those whom I hold dear,
the grace to fulfill perfectly thy holy will,
to accept for love of thee the joys
and sorrows of this passing life,
so that we may one day be
united together in heaven
for all eternity.

AMEN